The Little Conflict Ender

Project Credits

Cover and Interior Illustrations: Kai Pannen

Translation: Emily Banwell

Cover Design: Brian Dittmar Design, Inc.

Book Production: John McKercher

Copy Editor: Amy Bauman

Managing Editor: Alexandra Mummery

Publicity Coordinator: Martha Scarpati

Special Sales Manager: Judy Hardin

Rights Coordinator: Diane Gedymin

Customer Service Manager: Christina Sverdrup

Order Fulfillment: Washul Lakdhon

Administrator: Theresa Nelson

IT Support: Peter Eichelberger

Publisher: Kiran S. Rana

Stephanie Schneider

The Little Conflict Ender
A Family Guide to Working Things Out

With illustrations by Kai Pannen
Translated by Emily Banwell

Hunter House
PUBLISHERS

Turner Publishing Company
424 Church Street · Suite 2240 · Nashville, Tennessee 37219
445 Park Avenue · 9th Floor · New York, New York 10022
www.turnerpublishing.com

Library of Congress Cataloging-in-Publication Data
Schneider, Stephanie, 1972–
[Kleine Streitberater. English]
The little conflict ender : a family guide to working things out /
Stephanie Schneider ; with illustrations by Kai Pannen.
pages   cm
Originally published in German as: Der kleine Streitberater :
Familienkonflikte lösen mit Herz und Verstand, published by Kösel, 2013.
ISBN 978-0-89793-707-8 (cloth) — ISBN 978-0-89793-708-5 (ebook)
1. Families — Psychological aspects.   2. Interpersonal conflict.   I. Title.
HQ519.S36713 2014
158.2 — dc23   2014007708

Printed and bound by Friesens, Altona, Manitoba
Printed in Canada

9 8 7 6 5 4 3 2 1   First U.S. Edition   14 15 16 17 18

The goal is not to never fight again.
The goal is to make your fighting smarter.

Contents

Introduction

No, not every family fights. It is said that a couple of people somewhere in Wisconsin have never said an unkind word to each other. And legend has it that there's another extraordinary family like that in Arizona, too.

But everyone else fights. Some do it more than others. For some people, it stays at the level of harmless everyday conflicts, while others end up bitterly disappointed in family court. The vast majority of families probably fall somewhere in the middle.

I would place my own family somewhere in there, too. My family includes my husband, Jens, my two children, and me. For years, we have been getting into each others' hair with beautiful regularity, and the approaching signs of puberty suggest that the next few years probably won't be any calmer.

The four of us fight with great passion and stamina. But that doesn't mean we enjoy it. Oh, no. In fact, it's just as awful every time. And whenever the going gets tough for us, I often wish I had some kind of guide. I wish we had someone who would take me by the hand and remind me about all the useful ideas and tricks for

dealing with our conflicts that I always seem to forget in the heat of battle. In other words, I'm looking for a kind of conflict ender. This book probably won't help you avoid conflict altogether. But it aims to…

- …reassure you and remind you that you're not alone with this problem. In fact, you're in very good company!
- …help you gain a little perspective.
- …keep reminding you that the conflict has nothing to do with your qualifications as a father or mother. Good moms and dads fight, too—all of them!
- …give you a couple of suggestions and concrete tips.

Every family is different, and everyone fights differently. Try out some of the approaches here and see what you like. Maybe this collection will give you just the right tip to suit your family's needs.

Conflict Is Normal

My husband, Jens, and I used to try hard to keep anyone from noticing our constant fights with the children. The elaborate efforts we made! We even convinced our landlord to insulate the outer walls of the house, telling him the heating costs were too high for us. In fact, we were just trying to avoid the neighborhood knowing whenever our children were back to playing the "I'm doing something you don't want me to do" game.

But is it worth it to invest all that energy just to keep up appearances and pretend that everything's going swimmingly?

• • • Fighting is totally normal. • • •

Now, instead of hiding behind the refrigerated aisle in the grocery store every time we want to fight over the Monterey Jack or whatever cheese it might be, we've changed tactics. Our everyday lives go much more smoothly with the attitude, "Sorry! That's just the way we are!"

"Ever since we stopped spending so much time and energy on appearances, we have a lot of both left over—so we can come to an agreement."

Strong Children Fight

I admit it: Some days I would hand over my favorite pink purse to turn my children into a couple of easygoing model citizens. I'd love to have a pair of perfectly behaved third-graders who stay inside and study Picasso's biography even when the weather is gorgeous, rather than asking me, not without justification, "But what's it good for?" Other days I imagine them as gentle angels who politely thank Grandma for the flowered headband instead of sobbing that they specifically asked for the collector's album for the next World Cup.

Thank God all of my wishes don't come true as soon as I make them. Because what's the first thing a child does when she enters the world? She yells. And at that moment everyone in the room is thrilled about it. Why? Because at that moment it's a sign of liveliness and vitality to be yelling.

Sometimes making a fuss is really just the opposite of resignation and weakness. Strong children don't buckle under or sink into lethargy. They don't put up with just anything. Instead, they engage with the world, and sometimes they pound the table with their fists (and their sister's shins with their feet) when something seems unfair to them.

Still it can be pretty exhausting. That's why every family that faces conflicts head on, rather than trying to cover them up, deserves a medal.

> Parents who can handle conflict are priceless! Our children have very few places in their lives where they are allowed to be loud and inappropriate.

Fighting Is the Opposite of Complacency

Are you angry because your best friend doesn't have much time for you anymore? Are you upset because your son still hasn't started looking for an internship? Do you get angry with your wife when she forgets your anniversary? And do you think that conflict means your relationship is in crisis? On the contrary! The real crisis starts when you stop caring.

All of those annoying accusations and complaints tell the other person, "You're so important to me that I can get upset. If I'm fighting for something, that shows I care about it." So if you and your loved ones are always fighting, it doesn't automatically mean you're an unfriendly, heartless family. It can mean just the opposite. In fact, we are always fighting because we care so much about each other. In the words of the German actress Anna Thalbach: "Deep relationships require deep fights."

"Deep relationships require deep fights."

Are you someone who easily ends up in a debate? Congratulations! You're probably one of those people who take an interest in others' lives. Think about Nelson Mandela… or Pippi Longstocking, for that matter. They didn't exactly become famous by avoiding conflicts and big emotions.

Don't Fight with Just Anyone!

Let's be honest: fighting can be exhausting. Tears, quarrels, and grinding your teeth are all hard work. You need all of your strength to get through it. That's why you should fight only with people who are important to you. With anyone else, it's just a waste of time and energy! I just can't afford to fight with cashiers, cell phone service representatives, other people's children, political opponents, and the mothers in the athletic club all at the same time. After all, each day has only twenty-four hours, and during that time I also need to eat, be in love, feed the cat, lead the next climate change conference, or order another cappuccino. Every daily allowance of time and energy can be spent only once. So I have to decide: Which fights do I want to invest in, and which conflicts do I need to let go? Ideally, I should put the most work in places where I will benefit from the result:

- I'm going to work on my relationship with my husband instead of with my five hundred Facebook friends.
- I'll seek out the approval of my daughter rather than the gossipy women in my office.
- Instead of complaining about the lukewarm lasagna, I'm going to use my time in the restaurant today to have a long chat with my girlfriend.
- I'm going to debate the topic of "Is clearing the table child labor?" with my offspring rather than fighting a small-claims battle with our grouchy neighbors.

There's just no time to fight with boneheads and random strangers!

Am I Expecting Too Much?

We have some weeks when it seems my children and I just can't get along. Right now, for instance, I'm always fighting with my daughter. All it takes is a harmless "Do you want me to leave a few grapes for you?" for her to start rolling her eyes and making annoyed comments. Her upcoming math homework, the broken strap on her gym bag, or the weather forecast—nothing's too trivial to turn into a fight. How come?

"It's just the onset of puberty," says my mother, with a knowing look.

"It's because of how you raised her," says my friend, grinning.

"It's all nonsense," I say to myself, and then try a dose of self-criticism instead by asking myself if the real problem lies in me?

• • • **Maybe the real problem is with me?** • • •

How would I feel if I were in my children's shoes? Does my daughter have enough room left to grow in spite of all my expectations and instructions?

Imagine that you lived with someone who followed your every move. He knows your shoe size, makes decisions about your vacation plans, and chooses the day's menu. Hardly an evening goes by when you don't hear him pointing out what you could be doing better:

"Have you finished that annual report yet?"

"Don't eat so much bacon. Think about your cholesterol."

"Your colleague does Pilates. Don't you want to go with her sometime and see what you think?"

"Stop binge-watching *The Vampire Diaries*. You're going to rot your brain."

No one can possibly live up to all those demands. When I look at it that way, I can understand why my daughter sometimes flips her lid in response to my insistent tender loving care!

> If someone doesn't live up to my standards, that person can make an even greater effort. Or maybe I can lower my standards.

• • • Sometimes there's only one way out: Just breathe and let it go. • • •

17

Comfort for Squabblers

Why do we get upset with our partner for coming home too late? Why does Benny start kicking things when he doesn't get to play a game in his kindergarten class? And why is my friend always so bristly when we're talking about our attractive new colleague with the great job reviews? It's very simple.

We sometimes end up picking a fight when we…

- …feel we have been treated unfairly
- …are disappointed or dissatisfied
- …are afraid of not being loved anymore

There's a paradoxical truth in this because, often, the person picking a fight wants other people to be nice to them.

> Most of the time, the person picking a fight just wants other people to be nice to him or her.

Of course, this tactic doesn't work very well. Compliments would probably serve him much better than accusations. Nonetheless, we keep pursuing the same dubious strategy over and over again. That's why I committed the following sentence to memory and also wrote it on my bathroom mirror:

• • • People who pick fights are looking to be comforted! • • •

This thought doesn't make the people I encounter any friendlier. But it does make me feel calmer. In difficult situations, I remind myself why the other person is being aggressive—and my need to fight with that person suddenly disappears. Sometimes all of the air goes out of the fight as soon as I let go and accommodate the other person a little bit.

When Two People Fight, Everyone Joins In

The one thing we can all agree on is a bad mood. Whether it starts because one of the children didn't sleep well or because the cat is buggy with fleas, the battle cry "bad mood" causes everyone to join the fray. The only way to avoid being infected by the whinovirus is to take an active stand against it. The important question here:

• • • Is this really my fight? • • •

Do you just happen to be in the same room while your colleague is complaining, your husband is getting into his father-in-law's thinning hair, or your children are letting off some of their rainy-day energy? Are you really involved in this "car crash," or are you just an accidental witness? If you realize that you're just an onlooker, it's a good idea to stay out of it.

Here are some ways to do that:

- Grab some headphones and the vacuum cleaner and squeeze in a quick house-cleaning session with your favorite musical accompaniment.
- Go out and get some fresh air. Even five minutes will usually do it.
- Call a good friend on the spot and ask her to distract you with something cheerful.

Or you can try the vacation exercise on the following page.

The Vacation Exercise

Do you have the courage to look ridiculous sometimes? If so, the following exercise can help keep you from catching other people's bad moods.

Put on that big straw hat you bought last year on your trip to the beach. Officially designate it the "vacation hat." Promise yourself that this hat will make you immune to any kind of conflict, and that while you're wearing it, you will under no circumstances take part in the squabbling around you. From now on, a good-mood cloak surrounds you as soon as you put on the hat.

• • • The hat is your safe zone. • • •

Now pretend you're on vacation. Smile peacefully in the face of hissy fits and midlife crises. Your headwear is a clear reminder to you and the people around you: *Go ahead! Complain, whine, and fight, but I am not going to be a part of it! My mind is in a completely different place right now.*

After a while, just pointing at the hat and putting on a poker face will be enough to remind any sourpusses in the area not to expect any help from you. The vacation exercise works when you're away from home, too. Showing up in a big sombrero at work or soccer practice will lighten the mood with even the crabbiest of people.

Unfortunately, the hat exercise doesn't always work. Sometimes the prevailing bad mood is stronger than a vacation souvenir. If you feel yourself being pulled into the negative atmosphere, be sure to take the hat off before you get involved in the discussion. That way, the hat is still defined as a safe zone.

You don't necessarily need a hat for this exercise. Ski goggles, a sari, an old diving suit, or a shell necklace would work just as well. The main thing is for you to pick out something from a vacation that is easily visible on your body. The sillier and more obvious it is, the more effective it will be.

What Can I Do to Make You Feel Better?

It was a totally normal Saturday afternoon in April. I was taking full advantage of my day off by bellyaching and getting into fights with my family. I found myself standing in the kitchen, nagging them: "Why is someone's retainer in the butter dish?" "It's not my job to clean up after you. I bet the cat hasn't been fed yet, either." "And what about your report on the love life of the South American sloth?"

Right in the middle of my stream of complaints, Jens suddenly interrupted me, calm as a cucumber: "Hang on a minute, beloved woman and spousal partner. What can I do to make you feel better?" Agitated, I started to repeat my accusations about hungry retainers sneaking into

butter dishes and making abstract artwork. But Jens interrupted me and asked the question again: "Yes, I heard you. But what can I specifically do here and now to make you feel better?"

I thought for a second. And suddenly I heard myself saying, "I slept really badly last night, and I'm tired. I think I'd like to lie down for an hour." That was all? Was that the real reason I was ruining the weekend mood for all four of us?

Awestruck, I looked at my husband and silently repeated the magic formula to myself:

• • • What can I do right now, in this moment, to make you feel better? • • •

Was it possible that instead of cereal, Jens had eaten a bowl of pure wisdom for breakfast?

Within half an hour, he had gathered up the children and taken them out to do the grocery shopping for the rest of the week. I, on the other hand, lay in bed with a hot water bottle at my feet and a warm, cozy feeling in my heart.

I don't really want to share my husband, but I'm generous with his magic spells. You're welcome to use them, too.

23

Press "Pause"

What do a good yeast dough and a family conflict have in common? They both need to rest for a while in order to produce good results. Try pressing the "Pause" button the next time the waves get choppy and try one of these:

- Do some yoga or make the beds.
- Count to 10,306.
- Drink a cup of coffee.
- Call your best friend or do some quick repairs on the Honda.

The important thing is for you to take a break. That will greatly increase your chances of finding a good solution. After all, we're fighting because there is a problem and we want something to change. But the more upset we get, the less likely we are to find a solution.

Many small conflicts can be resolved just by letting a little time go by. And the really important problems? Well, they're still going to be there anyway. When it comes to the chronic conflicts in your life, an extra half hour isn't going to make a difference. When you realize it might be a good time for you to step back from actively engaging a problem, say:

• • • Let me think about it. • • •

Those five little words are a secret relaxation tip for parents and children. Use the sentence as a ringtone, write it on your children's vocabulary flash cards, and have them inoculated with it at their next tetanus booster—do whatever it takes to make sure someone will remember it at the crucial moment the next time you need to press pause. "I heard what you said. Let me think about it for a little bit, okay?"

Meltdowns Are Not the Same as Conflicts

If I have learned one thing from living with Jens and our two children, it's this: When it comes to building a harmonious family life, even eight-year-old kids have an equal vote. Naturally there are some distinctions, but if we're going to get along with the other three members of the family, we have to remember that we're all a team, and we all need to work together for it to feel right.

But wait! Do you have a two- or three-year-old? That's different. Remember:

• • • Meltdowns are not the same as conflict. • • •

During the terrible twos (and threes), children are in their own universe, living according to their own rules. When a child throws himself onto the ground at the supermarket checkout and starts shrieking, even the most logical argument will be pointless. You can't reason with a child who's going through the terrible twos. You just have to get through it, take deep breaths, and make sure your child doesn't pull a pot of boiling water off the stove or meet with some other disaster during one of those fits.

When it comes to serious meltdowns, the wait-and-see approach is best. Save your valuable child-rearing approaches and clever arguments. There's nothing you can do right now anyway. Believe me; time is on your side.

> You can expect a child in elementary school to be considerate and understand certain things. It's different with a child in the terrible twos.

Conflict Is Good...

By now, everyone in our debate-loving family understands that conflict is normal and healthy. But where is my limit? I can define my personal boundaries by asking the following question:

• • • Will this fight ultimately make my life better or worse? • • •

Conflict makes my life worse when…

- …we are just nagging and complaining without knowing why or when we ruin a good mood and the chance for a couple of pleasant hours for no good reason
- …someone is consistently being put at a disadvantage or humiliated
- …the fight harms my relationship with my husband or the children rather than strengthening us and increasing our ability to deal with conflict
- …the fight makes the problem bigger rather than bringing us closer to a solution

...but Escalation Is Bad

Conflict makes my life better when...

- ...it helps me finally overcome my weaker self and face a problem that I would normally avoid
- ...it wakes me up and makes me listen to someone whose problems I was overlooking
- ...our children realize that these scenes are part of normal life and that such conflicts will also go away
- ...making up afterward gives us the feeling of being closer than before
- ...it shows that everyone in our family can express an opinion and that there can be good arguments for both sides

"Loud noise doesn't always mean something is being destroyed. Sometimes what you're hearing is the noise from a construction project that will build a better future."

Give Peter a Hand

Grown-ups aren't exactly crazy about fights and bad moods, but they can usually evaluate how serious the other person's outbursts are. It can be very different for children, as the following example shows.

Peter is six years old, and he works for a company known as "The Family." One day he is sitting in his room, as usual, trying to focus on a complicated Lego structure, when his ears suddenly perk up. Uh oh. The big bosses in the office next door are really getting into it. There's no way to ignore the yelling.

Peter would like to know what's going on. Unfortunately, though, they're speaking grown-up language to each other, and it sounds like Chinese to his ears. That means he can't tell whether it is just a harmless exchange of words or whether this is the big one and the company is about to go bankrupt.

Little Peter starts to panic, which is only fair—after all, he has a lot at stake here. He is dependent on the big bosses, and he has invested a lot of time and emotion into The Family in the last few years.

The craziest thoughts run through his mind. Did he do something wrong on the job? Did he give them the wrong calculations or forget to pass on an important message? Peter has trouble sleeping that night. His brain is working overtime, but since he doesn't speak Chinese, he doesn't get anywhere. Poor Peter...

Peter Is Worried

We, as adults, can easily forget that children are very sensitive when it comes to conflict. Sometimes even harmless debates can seem very intense to them. When that happens, children worry more than they need to or even blame themselves for things that have nothing to do with them.

Peter Responds Quietly

Some children are not afraid to speak up, and they tell everyone from their great-uncle to the cashier how they feel, loudly and clearly. But not everyone can do that. Kids such as Peter process things a little more slowly and quietly, so it's a good idea to take a closer look every so often.

Help Peter Get a Better Understanding of Things

As the "CEO," it's your responsibility to go into Peter's office after a fight and talk to him—even if the fight seemed totally harmless to you. Always let your employees know what was going on, and reassure them that the company's balance sheets and jobs are not in danger.

Time-Outs

But what do you do when one thing leads to another and the mood just keeps getting worse and worse, with no constructive solution in sight? Our family has a special time-out ritual for these kinds of situations. The advantage of this exercise is that one person is not labeled as being at fault and sent to his or her room or to the corner. Instead, everyone contributes to the family's sense of calm.

What's also handy is that it works for the fight of the century just as well as it does for little everyday arguments.

This is how the time-out exercise works:

- When someone realizes a fight is escalating, he or she pulls the emergency brake and loudly and clearly says, "Time-out!" Adults as well as children can make this announcement. It also doesn't matter whether the person calling the time out is one of the people fighting or is completely uninvolved.
- A time-out call must always be followed. Do not debate whether or not a time out is appropriate in this particular situation.
- Everyone in the room stops what he or she is doing. Conversations are immediately put on hold. Nobody does anything other than taking a time-out.
- Each person finds a room where he or she can be alone. That includes people who weren't involved in the fight.

- The time-out lasts five minutes. I normally set an egg timer and put it in the hallway before I disappear into my time-out room.
- When the egg timer goes off, anyone who wants to come back is allowed to. Those who have been distracted by the latest Spider-Man comic book in the meantime or feel as if they need more time to cool off, simply stay where they are.

That's it. You don't need any other rules. Your migraine will still keep pounding after a time-out. Your children won't start angelically doing their homework, and your husband still won't be a fan of spending Christmas with his mother-in-law. Nonetheless, your interactions will most likely be changed in some way.

Our children are happy to go along with this ritual now that they've realized they can call a time-out, too, and they demand absolute obedience from the grown-ups.

My tip: Don't underestimate your children! Be prepared for them to interrupt you right in the middle of the juiciest fight with your spouse. After all, they can usually tell exactly when it's time for a time-out, and they will interrupt you mercilessly. And then you will have to follow the rules too, without exception:

> No discussions. Apply the emergency brake. Five minutes of quiet time for everyone.

Avoid Presidential-Style Debates

Is the general mood at an all-time low, and you're arguing yourselves into a corner? Then take a step back and ask yourself, "What's happening here? Are we fighting to be acknowledged? Are we looking for a compromise? Or are we just in a bad mood and don't know what to do about it?"

• • • Are we fighting to come to an agreement or to win? • • •

You're probably familiar with the presidential debates that are always aired during election season. Of course the candidates are not trying to reach an agreement. The only purpose of those events is to show who can keep the upper hand during all the mudslinging.

Stop fighting and start agreeing! Why should we hold a presidential-style debate if it's not going to get us to the goal? Would you go to work if you didn't get paid for it? Would you have surgery on your nose to fix your fallen arches? The only way to counteract this tendency is with facts, facts, and more facts.

The next page shows you an easy way to get at those essential facts.

Sometimes a piece of paper can help keep you from getting bogged down in the details. Write down the subject of the conflict; for instance, "physics homework" or "hair in the bathtub" or "the account is overdrawn" or "you keep looking at me funny." Let's choose a random topic: "We won the lottery. What should we do with the money?" Put the piece of paper in the middle of the table. Then write down all of your options, either individually or as a group. For example:

- Save it all.
- Donate it all.
- Spend $30,000 on shoes, donate $30,000, and invest the rest in the stock market.
- Ask Uncle Harry. He's good with money.
- Take a vote.
- Ignore the windfall and keep living the way we have always lived.

Write down the first three or four possible solutions that come to mind. It doesn't matter whether they are completely ridiculous or absolutely realistic. Without thinking about it too hard, underline the answer you think is the best. Then try to stick to it and be consistent!

Naturally you can't solve major arguments with just a sheet of paper. But when the goal is lying there in the middle of the table, within reach, it's much easier to solve the problem than to get caught up in a presidential-style debate.

• • • Fight for something, not against something. • • •

Sibling Conflicts

This heading will come as no surprise to anyone who lives with children. Why do siblings enjoy antagonizing each other so much? If you believe my husband, Jens, it's a special kind of training. He says,

> "Parents teach you the theory of life. Siblings are the sparring partners who help you put the theory to the test for the first time."

It makes sense, and who is better suited for this than your little brother or big sister? They can't threaten you with things like, "Then I won't invite you to my birthday party" or "Then you're not my friend anymore." Besides, your own family is wonderfully convenient. A sibling is much more readily available than your pen pal in Australia or the boys from your hockey team.

So what could be more natural than practicing your conflict training and social skills right there at home as you brush your teeth or in the car during the next long, boring ride? In this way, our children arrange a training schedule of their own that makes pro athletes' schedules pale by comparison.

So far, so good. But that's exactly the sticking point:

> Sports are not healthy per se, and fighting isn't necessarily good for you in and of itself.

That's why I set the following rules for us and for our children:

1. Siblings are allowed to fight.

   Mom and Dad have to put up with it. They can't roll their eyes and threaten to take away your tickets to the game or serve stuffed peppers for dinner every time a good fight gets underway. But that doesn't automatically mean brothers and sisters can do whatever they want to each other. After all…

2. Younger and weaker siblings were not invented so that the other person would have someone to polish their ego.

And last but not least, it is a matter of how they treat each other:

3. The stronger one is welcome to feel superior and enjoy the situation to its fullest, but he or she should not constantly point it out!

   Even if the power struggles between siblings are clearly inevitable and natural, no one deserves to hear, "You can't do that anyway" or "You're so dumb" or "Go away; you're bugging me" all day long. Even if it's true.

Figure It Out Yourselves!

"It's so unfair," says my child when he gets home from school. "First the teachers say we're supposed to tell them if someone is bothering us. But when you go to the principal, they send you away and say, 'You need to figure it out for yourselves.'"

Sigh. There are obviously some classic child-rearing phrases that are handed down from generation to generation. One of those is "Figure it out yourselves." I heard that one when I was six, too. Back then, I was being bullied by Alex and his secret schoolyard gang. I screwed up my courage and went to the teacher on duty. But the only thing she said was, "You can figure it out for yourselves. You're not babies anymore."

And why not? What's wrong with telling children they can do things for themselves? After all, it's good if adults don't get involved, right? Theoretically, yes. But the other side of the coin is the fact that children are going to adults and asking them for help. Obviously they don't know what else to do.

Fighting is an incredibly complicated thing. It's something that has to be learned. So why shouldn't children ask their parents, teachers, and guardians for help? We were perfectly willing to help them learn to swim, ride a bike, and do long division, after all.

If we get involved, it doesn't automatically mean trying to make everything easy for the kids who are fighting. For instance, if my child comes sobbing to me and says, "Mommy, Belinda in my class broke my ruler, and she keeps stealing the salami out of my sandwich during recess," she certainly doesn't want me to show up at her school the next day and give Belinda a good talking to. But she would probably be very grateful for a little encouragement and some tips on how to resolve the situation herself.

Don't just tell children to solve their own conflicts. Instead, tell them **how** to do it.

And that's the key part, because let's be honest: Do we even know what to tell our children when it comes to battling the Belindas of the world? Or are we sending them away because we're busy and we don't really know, either?

Sometimes the phrase "You need to figure it out yourselves" really means "I can't deal with your problem."

My Mediation Technique for Moms and Dads

What do I do when yet another sibling battle is raging and my children are loudly demanding that I act as the mediator? Over the last few years, I have gotten countless great-sounding tips from parenting magazines, neighbors, and television shows on TLC, but none of them really helped. So I had to do some experimenting on my own.

The following ritual is my own personal mediation tactic. It's so simple, in fact, that even I don't understand why it works so well. I tell my children that I am not going to give them the answers; I am here to help them figure it out for themselves.

> Tell your children: "I'm not going to give you the answers. I am here to help you figure it out yourselves."

Let's take an everyday situation, the kind of thing that happens a dozen times a day: Imagine that Ben and Nina are having another fight. Ben wants the flashlight, but it's in Nina's room. Nina tells Ben he cannot come into her room. They start arguing, wrestling by the bedroom door, and loudly yelling for me to come solve the argument. Here's what you do:

1. Get one of the children to tell you what happened.

Say to the children, "It doesn't matter who goes first, since you both get a turn." Pick one child and say, "So I'm going to start with you. What's going on?"

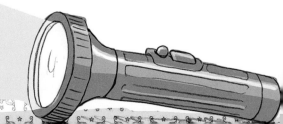

Tell the other child: "It'll be your turn next, and then you'll have a chance to talk, too."

2. Give the other child a chance to explain what happened.

"Now it's your turn," you say to the other child. "What made you so upset?"

3. Summarize what you have heard and ask for feedback.

"What I heard was this: You didn't want Ben to go into your room. And Ben, you don't want Nina to grab you and shove you. Is that right? Did I understand you both correctly?"

Often, a lot of the anger evaporates when both of them have a chance to explain things calmly.

4. Help the children find a solution.

Often, the solution is very simple: Both children promise to do what the other one wants.

"So you heard what the other person wanted. Is that all right with you? You'll give him the flashlight and stop hitting him, and in exchange he'll stay away from your room?"

(The mediator tactic continues on the next page.)

In most cases, the fight dissolves into thin air at this point. Now can you see why I'm so amazed by how simple this method is? Is it because I'm speaking very calmly and have a grave look on my face? Because the children feel like they're being taken seriously? I have no idea.

Of course it doesn't always work that smoothly. Sometimes we have to look for other solutions.

5. Look for alternatives.

"What are some other ways you could come to an agreement? It looks like both of you are going to have to compromise."

If the children can't come up with anything after thinking about it for a little while, then I make a suggestion. Depending on the subject of the fight, I might say, "Would it be all right if you traded off every five minutes?"

or

"Can you give him something else instead?"

or

"Do you have another suggestion?"

6. Ending without an agreement.

What if the children don't go for any of my suggestions? I don't keep fighting for them to find a solution. After all, this fight isn't my problem! As a rule, when that happens I say, as calmly as possible, "It looks to me like there's no solution right now."

At those times, my children learn a valuable lesson: If someone boycotts the negotiations, they can't move forward. I look at the more cooperative of the two and say, "I'm sorry, but when someone decides to be stubborn, it doesn't matter how hard we try—we aren't going to find a good solution. There's nothing we can do about it right now."

Sometimes I have the feeling that this statement does more good for my children than any of the compromises we've hammered out. Sometimes I also make a decision over my children's heads at this point in order to resolve the situation. For instance, I might take away the thing they were fighting over and keep it for a specified length of time.

There's another thing that works well: Don't force an immediate agreement! Sometimes the other person can't give in right away because that would mean losing face. Often, the situation is resolved five minutes later once no one is watching them anymore.

"Maybe you just need to give Nina a little time, Ben. Then she might decide to give you the flashlight after all."

You've given them some help, and now it's time to step back. Then the children have a chance to resolve the situation themselves after they've taken a short break.

"Sometimes the heart just needs more time than the brain!"

Water under the Bridge

Is it time for a reconciliation? Congratulations. But don't ruin your peace offering by attaching conditions to it. Consistent parents are great, but this is not the right time for it. The most important first step is to get along. Everything else can be handled later.

••• See things from your child's perspective, again and again. •••

Many parents are afraid of losing face if they forgive and forget too quickly after a family fight. They wonder, "Won't my child keep acting up in the future if I don't give him the cold shoulder for a while, after what he just did?" But that's an unnecessary fear.

When it comes to your children, you don't need to do battle with them. The reason is very simple: because you are the parents. For your children, you are a natural authority and the yardstick for everything else. Yes, it's true—even when your offspring is doing everything possible to prove the opposite. So relax your battle-scarred self-confidence and believe in yourself!

> Parents who do battle with their children and win the fight have actually lost.

Instead, imagine yourself as a mirror. Everything that your children see in it, they transfer to themselves. What would it be like if your kids looked in the parental mirror and saw the message below?

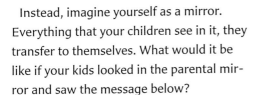

"Don't worry; fighting is normal, and it can't threaten our relationship. No matter how upset we are with each other, one thing is for sure: You will never lose my love, and I am always ready to make up with you."

Children who experience forgiveness despite all of their mistakes and quirks will be able to forgive themselves and others as adults, too. As my old friend Mahatma Gandhi once said, "The weak can never forgive. Forgiveness is the attribute of the strong." So go ahead; set a good example. Show your strength. Put yourself in the other person's shoes and make them a peace offering.

43

Celebrate Reconciliations

Reconciliation is a big word. Naturally, not everyone is willing to fall into the other person's arms with stammered explanations and grand gestures. But you don't need a big gesture to acknowledge a little bit of peace. You can do it without words or guitar serenades.

Fortunately you can find plenty of other ways to say that things are back to normal. Reconciliation rituals can be helpful. They are important because they soothe the soul. Sometimes you can feel pretty exhausted after one of those thundering family storms, and your emotions could use a little healing balm. So why not really celebrate your reconciliation? People who manage to finish a fight deserve a reward.

Our family loves it when we…
- …go out to eat
- …plan a family TV-watching or game night
- …make banana pancakes
- …hug
- …go for a walk together after dinner and stop at the ice cream shop

Reconciliations can take just as long as the fight that preceded them. If we spent all Sunday morning sniping at each other over the stains on the new leather couch, we get to take the whole afternoon off to smoke the peace pipe together. If Jens and I have a twenty-minute debate about his driving skills on the way home, that's exactly how long we get to spend on a coffee break at the rest stop.

Getting along means much more than just not continuing a fight. Reconciliation is an art, but it doesn't require red roses or diamond rings. You can do something completely normal and declare it to be a peace ritual. "All right, now we're going to have a nice make-up dinner," you can say, and then sit down together at the table as usual. That's enough, but it's really up to you. Your imagination is the only limit.

Here are some ideas you can try; I'm sure you will have many of your own.

- Did you have a fight over breakfast? Have a symbolic exchange of scarves (or some other thing that they both find meaningful) before you leave the house.
- Is your son much too cool to talk with you? Grab your cell phone and text him from the next room: "I'm glad you're not mad anymore! Let me know if you want help with your math. Mom."
- Or do you prefer the grand gesture? Throw open all of the windows and have everyone sweep out the rest of the "bad air," waving your hands wildly.

Most children love celebrating like this in their everyday lives. Most grown-ups are the same way, actually, even if they're not usually aware of it. The crazier the ritual, the faster your subconscious gets it: "Oh, thank God—the storm has passed. Everything is easy and good again."

It Is Just a Matter of Time until the Next Conflict

Washing the dishes is usually a pretty straightforward task. You put water in the sink, start with a dirty plate or bowl, and work through the pile one piece at a time. Eventually, it's done and everything is clean. It's a good feeling.

Conflicts aren't quite that easy. Unfortunately, it's rare that you can pick up each piece of the fight individually, wash and dry it by hand, hang up the dishtowel to dry, and then say, "There; done. All of our misunderstandings and disagreements are gone. We can put our clean, straightforward agreement on the shelf." That good feeling of being completely done with a conflict is sadly very rare—partly because the next fight is usually waiting in the wings while you're still negotiating the peace treaty for the last one.

Fighting is a process that follows us our whole lives long. That means you probably won't read this book once and then put it away; instead, you'll want to pick it up and consult it every so often. Think of it as your conflict assistant, a source of ideas, even a guide through stormy times.

However you see this book, may it help you. And here's wishing you a good journey and plenty of fun with your reconciliations.

> "The best thing about fighting is the feeling you have afterward: Our relationship can handle this."

The Author

Stephanie Schneider is a freelance journalist and the author of the bestselling book *Warum Mama eine rosa Handtasche braucht* (Why Mama Needs a Pink Purse). She lives in a thin-walled apartment building in Hanover, Germany, with her husband, two children, and three crazy gerbils. Schneider's motto: Only write about things you know really well. That means when it comes to dealing with conflicts, she recommends only those ideas she has successfully tried out herself.
www.stephanie-schneider.de

The Illustrator

Kai Pannen studied painting and film in Cologne, Germany. He has worked as an illustrator and animator since 1990. He regularly illustrates books, including the successful "Oscar the Sheep" books *Kopf Hoch!* (Cheer Up!) and *Nur Mut!* (Be Brave!) for Kösel-Verlag. Pannen lives and works in Hamburg, Germany.
www.kaipannen.de

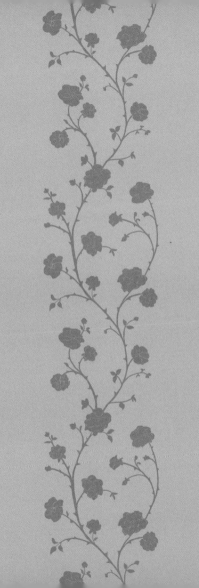